**HEINEMANN
STATE STUDIES**

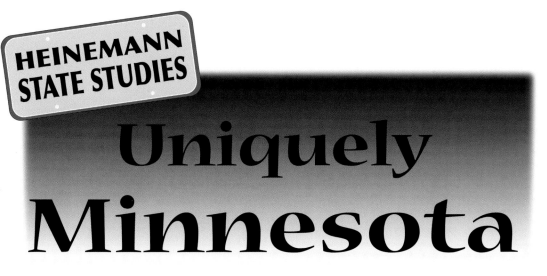

Uniquely
Minnesota

Stephanie Ash

Heinemann Library
Chicago, Illinois

Designed by Heinemann Library
Printed in China by WKT Company Limited.

08 07 06 05 04
10 9 8 7 6 5 4 3 2 1

**Library of Congress
Cataloging-in-Publication Data**

Ash, Stephanie Wilbur, 1974–
  Uniquely Minnesota / Stephanie Wilbur Ash.
    p. cm.—(State studies)
Summary: Provides an overview of various aspects
of Minnesota that make it a unique state, including
its people, land, government, culture, economy,
and attractions.

Includes bibliographical references and index.
  ISBN 1-4034-4494-3 (lib. bdg.)—
ISBN 1-4034-4509-5 (pbk.)
  1. Minnesota—Juvenile literature. [1. Minnesota.]
I. Title. II. Series.
  F606.3.A84 2003
  977.6—dc21
                          2003008983

Acknowledgments
Development and photo research by
BOOK BUILDERS LLC

The author and publishers are grateful to the
following for permission to reproduce copyright
material:

Cover photographs by (top, L–R) Macduff Everton/
Corbis; Joseph Sohm, ChromoSohm Inc./Corbis;
20-20 Photographic; Brett Patterson/Corbis;
(main) Courtesy Minnesota Office of Tourism

Title page (L–R) Courtesy Minnesota Office of
Tourism; Courtesy Minnesota Office of Tourism;
Stock Connection, Inc./Alamy; Contents page Paul
Stafford/Minnesota Office of Tourism; p. 4 Jon P.
Yeager/Corbis; pp. 8, 9T, 10, 13T, 13L, 13R, 14T,
15B, 21B, 23, 24, 30, 40 Courtesy Minnesota
Office of Tourism; p. 5, 37 Stock Connection, Inc./
Alamy; pp. 8B, 43, 45 IMA for Book Builders, LLC;
pp. 9B, 20, 29, 39 Paul Stafford/Minnesota Office
of Tourism; p. 11T Joseph Sohm, ChromoSohm
Inc./Corbis; p. 15T Courtesy of Buena Vista Gem
Works; p. 16 Hulton/Getty Images; p. 17 Steve
Skjold/Alamy; p. 18 Culver Pictures; pp. 21T, 22T
POPPERFOTO/Alamy; p. 22B Erick S. Lesser/Getty
Images; pp. 25, 34, 38, 41B Andre Jenny/Alamy;
p. 26 Michael Smith/Getty Images; p. 28 Courtesy
Minnesota State Fair; p. 31 Foodfolio/Alamy; p. 33
Courtesy Runestone Museum; p. 35 Elsa/Getty
Images; p. 36 20-20 Photographic; p. 41T Brett
Patterson/Corbis; p. 42 Macduff Everton/Corbis.

Special thanks to Matthew Mauch of Minnesota
State University, Mankato, for his expert comments
in the preparation of this book.

Every effort has been made to contact copyright
holders of any material reproduced in this book.
Any omissions will be rectified in subsequent
printings if notice is given to the publisher.

Cover Pictures

Top (left to right) Cross-country skiers,
Minnesota state flag, high school hockey
player, Spoonbridge and Cherry sculpture
Main Lake Country in Minnesota

Some words are shown in bold, **like this.**
You can find out what they mean by looking
in the glossary.

Contents

Uniquely Minnesota

*U*nique means to be special, uncommon. A place can be unique, too. Minnesota is unique. The large number of lakes—about 12,000 of them—make the state unique. The millions of acres of forests and wilderness protected by the government make Minnesota unique. And the cold winters—some of the coldest winter temperatures in the United States—make Minnesota unique.

ORIGINS OF THE STATE'S NAME

"Minnesota" is a Dakota word meaning "sky-tinted waters." That is what the Dakota people called the Mississippi River. But the name also refers to the thousands of lakes in Minnesota. Minnesota has more lakes than any other state, except Alaska.

MAJOR CITIES

Minnesota also is unique because of its two largest cities, Minneapolis and St. Paul. These cities are so close together that visitors sometimes do not know where one city stops and the other starts. People call them the Twin Cities.

The capital of Minnesota is St. Paul, which is in the east-central part of the state. The city used to be called Pig's

More than 10,000 years ago, mile-thick glaciers, which are giant sheets of moving ice, melted over Minnesota and created the lakes and rivers.

Eye after Pig's Eye Parrant, a settler with only one good eye. He came up the Mississippi River from Iowa. He built the first shack in what is now St. Paul in around 1838. Others soon followed, and the name was changed to St. Paul to honor the first church built there. The church was named after Saint Paul, the favorite saint of the French priest, Lucien Galtier, who built the church.

In 1848 St. Paul became the capital of the Minnesota Territory and in 1858 its state capital.

This Mississippi River town started as a center for fur trading. Men trapping beaver, fox, and rabbit for furs would come to the area to trade the furs for money and supplies. When the city was named as the state capital, it quickly grew as the center for the state's government. Today, about 280,000 people live in St. Paul.

Minneapolis is Minnesota's largest city, with about 382,000 people. It is just across the Mississippi River and to the west of its twin city, St. Paul. The city grew from a settlement near a large waterfall on the Mississippi River. The falls provided power for log and flour mills. City leaders named the city Minneapolis, a combination of the Native American word "minne," which means water, and the Greek word "polis," which means city.

DULUTH

The **port** city of Duluth is on the southwestern edge of Lake Superior in northeastern Minnesota. It is the busiest freshwater port in North America. Cargo ships travel through the Great Lakes to Duluth carrying products from all over the world. They carry goods out of Duluth too, including timber and **iron ore** from Minnesota's mines.

Minnesota's Geography and Climate

Minnesota is in the north-central part of the United States. To the north is Canada, and to the south is Iowa. Wisconsin borders the state on the east, and North and South Dakota are to the west. Minnesota is the twelfth-largest state.

LAND

Minnesota has four major land regions. Rolling plains, deep woods, and high **bluffs** can all be found in Minnesota. Farmland and prairies cover a small southwestern corner of the state known as the Dissected Till

The Northwest Angle

A **peninsula** in Canada is really part of Minnesota. This peninsula, called the Northwest Angle, is the northernmost point in the United States, except for Alaska. The Northwest Angle is not connected to the United States by land. A lake called the Lake of the Woods nearly surrounds the Northwest Angle, so the only way to drive to the peninsula is to go through Canada. Only about 100 people live on the Northwest Angle, but many visitors come to fish, hunt, boat, hike, ride snowmobiles, and enjoy the birds and wildlife.

Lake Effect

One place where temperatures are not so extreme is near Lake Superior. Minnesotans call the unique weather near Lake Superior the Lake Effect. Because the lake's water temperature stays the same—40°F year-round—the air around the lake is cooler in the summer and warmer in the winter than the rest of Minnesota. Average daily temperatures along Lake Superior range from 62°F in summer to 13°F in winter. It also snows more near Lake Superior than in the rest of the state, due to water vapor blown off the lake by easterly winter winds. The annual snowfall averages about 55 inches near the lake.

Plains. In the Young Drift Plain, farmland and prairies cover the northwestern part of the state along the Red River. In the northern part of the state, the Superior Upland is thick with birch and pine trees and dotted with lakes, some linked together like chains. Minnesota's highest point, Eagle Mountain at 2,301 feet above sea level, is located here. Though most of Minnesota is fairly flat, the Driftless Area in the southeast corner is known for gently rolling hills that turn into steep bluffs that rise above the Mississippi and St. Croix rivers.

CLIMATE

Sometimes hot, sometimes cold, sometimes snowy, sometimes rainy, sometimes dry—that is Minnesota's weather, or climate. The weather is **extreme.** It changes often and fast.

In the summer, temperatures usually range from 70° to 90°F but can reach 100°F or more. The air can also be **humid,** which can make it feel even hotter.

In the winter, temperatures usually range from 32°F to well below zero but can fall as low as –20 or –30°F. Minnesota's winter temperatures are some of the coldest in the **continental** United States. In fact, Minnesota's coldest temperature on record is among the top five coldest

Minnesota's snowiest winter came in 1983–1984, when the state received more than 98 inches of snow.

temperatures recorded in the United States. According to the National Climatic Data Center, the official coldest temperature in Minnesota was –60°F in the town of Tower on February 2, 1996. But the town of Embarrass holds the unofficial record on that same day in February. Officials say it was –65°F there.

SNOW AND RAIN

Snowfall across Minnesota can be heavy. In an average year, between 40 and 50 inches of snow will fall in one winter—the same height as a fourth-grade student. The record snowfall for one twenty-four hour period was set on October 31–November 1, 1991, in the Twin Cities. Twenty-one inches of snow fell—that is about as high as a fire hydrant.

The eastern part of the state receives the greatest amount of precipitation. The amount decreases steadily toward the northwestern part of the state.

In Minnesota it rains most often in April, May, and September. An average year will bring 20 to 30 inches of rain.

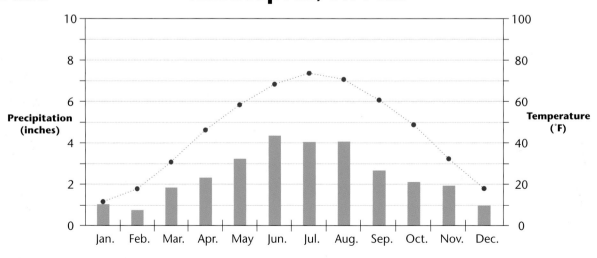

Minneapolis/St. Paul

Famous Firsts

Fond du Lac Tribal and Community College is a Minnesota community college, but it also is a tribal college that teaches and promotes the language, culture, and history of the Ojibwe people of Minnesota. It was founded in 1987. It is the only college of its kind in the United States.

The **Basilica** of St. Mary in Minneapolis is the first basilica built in the United States. It was started in 1907 and completed in 1926.

Three sports were invented in Minnesota. Ralph Samuelson was only eighteen years old when he bent pine boards into the first water skis in 1922. Three Minnesotans built the first snowmobile near Roseau in 1955. In 1980 hockey-playing Min-

Inline skating started as good summer practice for the winter sports of hockey and cross-country skiing. Today, it is a sport of its own.

Lake City, Minnesota, is the birthplace of waterskiing. The lake in Lake City, Lake Pepin, is not really a lake but a slow-flowing part of the Mississippi River.

Minneapolis' skyway system connects more than 52 city blocks.

nesota brothers made the first Rollerblade skates in the basement of their parents' home in Minneapolis.

The world's longest skyway system is in Minneapolis. Skyways are indoor walkways above ground. About seven miles of skyways connect most of the downtown buildings of Minneapolis. Because the weather in Minnesota can be so cold, these downtown skyways help people work, eat, and shop without ever going outside.

Minnesota had the first public bus in the United States. It transported miners from Hibbing to Alice in 1914 for fifteen cents a ride. That one bus line grew into Greyhound bus lines, serving more than 2,600 destinations across the country.

The first open-heart surgery in the nation was done in Minnesota in 1952. Two University of Minnesota surgeons sewed up a hole in the heart of a five-year-old girl.

Snickers and Three Musketeers candy bars were made first in Minnesota by candy-maker Frank C. Mars. They were invented in the 1930s and sold for about five cents.

The first pop-up toaster was made in Minnesota. It was called the Toastmaker and was first sold in 1926 by McGraw Electric Company in Minneapolis for $13.30.

Minnesota's State Symbols

MINNESOTA STATE FLAG

In the middle of the Minnesota state flag is the state seal. On a red banner in the seal is the state motto, *Etoile du Nord,* which means "star of the north." That is what French **settlers** called the land that was Minnesota. Three dates important in Minnesota's history are woven into the flowered wreath on the flag. One is 1858, the year Minnesota became a state. One is 1819, the year the state's first military fort was built. And one is 1893, the year the flag was adopted. Nineteen stars on the flag show that Minnesota was the nineteenth state to enter the **Union.**

The largest star on the Minnesota state flag is at the top of the flag and stands for the North Star State, one of Minnesota's many nicknames.

MINNESOTA STATE SEAL

Minnesota's state seal is a **symbol** of cultures coming together. The seal shows two people on the banks

The Minnesota state seal has been used since Minnesota became a state in 1858.

11

of St. Anthony Falls, a center for travel and industry in the early days of the state. The Native American man on a horse and the barefoot farmer plowing the land represent two groups of people important to Minnesota's history. A tree stump with an ax shows the importance of logging in Minnesota's early days. Leaning against the stump is a **musket,** which stands for the pioneer spirit needed to live in wild, rugged Minnesota.

"Hail! Minnesota"

Minnesota, hail to thee!

Hail to thee, our state so dear,

Thy light shall ever be

A beacon bright and clear.

Thy son and daughters true

Will proclaim thee near and far,

They shall guard thy fame and adore thy name;

Thou shalt be their Northern Star.

Like the stream that bends to sea,

Like the pine that seeks the blue;

Minnesota, still for thee

Thy sons are strong and true.

From the woods and waters fair;

From the prairies waving far,

At thy call they throng with their shout and song;

Hailing thee their Northern Star.

STATE NICKNAME: LAND OF 10,000 LAKES

Minnesota is called the Land of 10,000 Lakes. But it is also called the North Star State, the Bread and Butter State for its wheat and dairy industries, and the Land of Sky-blue Waters. Minnesota is also called the **Gopher** State because of the many gophers found in southern Minnesota. A kind of **stoic** politeness in the face of anything is so popular among Minnesotans, and so made fun of, that it has earned the nickname Minnesota Nice.

STATE SONG: "HAIL! MINNESOTA"

University of Minnesota college students wrote a patriotic song called "Hail! Minnesota" in 1904 for a class play. Forty years later it became the official state song.

State Flower: Pink-and-White Lady Slipper

The pink-and-white lady slipper has been Minnesota's state flower since 1902. In Minnesota it grows best in shady marshes. To grow, the pink-and-white lady slipper needs a tiny **fungus** to help its roots get food from the soil.

State Tree: Red Pine

The red pine has been Minnesota's state tree since 1953. It is important in Minnesota because many red pines grow throughout the state and are cut for lumber. The tree can grow to nearly 100 feet tall, rarely gets sick, and lives for hundreds of years.

State Bird: Loon

Since 1961 the official state bird has been the loon. Loons look like large, black and white ducks. They swim, dive, and fish in Minnesota's northern lakes. Their call is a spooky

More than 12,000 loons live in Minnesota.

The pink-and-white lady slipper grows slowly—it may take twenty years before it flowers.

The red pine gets its name from the red-brown color of its bark.

The Other State Bird

Minnesotans would say there are two Minnesota state birds: the loon and the mosquito. Mosquitoes are not birds—they are insects—but they do fly. And they bite. Going outside during the summer may require protection from them. Mosquitoes need still, shallow water to breed. Because of the many lakes, mosquitoes are more of a problem in Minnesota than in other states.

The monarch butterfly, also known as the milkweed butterfly, changes several times throughout its life cycle. They migrate south every winter.

hoot that can be heard at great distances. The bird is even named for this call. "Loon" is a Norwegian word for "wild, sad cry."

STATE BUTTERFLY: MONARCH

The black, white, and orange monarch has been the Minnesota state butterfly since 2000. Many monarchs are born in Minnesota and then fly to Mexico for the winter.

STATE FISH: WALLEYE

The walleye has been the state fish of Minnesota since 1965. Walleyes live in cool water—60°F or less—so they like Minnesota's deep lakes.

STATE GEMSTONE: LAKE SUPERIOR AGATE

The Lake Superior **agate** has been Minnesota's state gemstone since 1969. The orange and red stripes that run through the white **quartz** come

The walleye can grow up to three feet long.

from the iron found in the soil of central and northeastern Minnesota.

STATE GRAIN: WILD RICE

Wild rice was a food staple grown by Native Americans long before it became the state grain in 1977. For many years, the world's entire supply of wild rice was grown in Minnesota.

Lake Superior agates can be found on the Iron Range of Minnesota. Polished Lake Superior agates can be made into jewelry.

STATE MUFFIN: BLUEBERRY

Minnesota is unique in that it has a state muffin: blueberry. Blueberries grow wild in late summer in northeast Minnesota. The muffin was adopted in 1988.

STATE MUSHROOM: MOREL

Minnesota's state mushroom, the morel, is a spongy mushroom that can be found in Minnesota's woods, ditches, and groves. Hunting for morels is a springtime tradition for many Minnesotans. It has been the state's mushroom since 1984.

The morel mushroom is an expensive delicacy that can cost more than $100 per pound.

Minnesota's History and People

Native Americans lived in Minnesota before Europeans arrived to farm and live on the land. Minnesota's harsh climate has kept some people away from the state, but the fertile land has brought many more.

EARLY CULTURE

Thousands of years ago almost all of Minnesota was covered with **glaciers.** When the ice melted nearly 10,000 years ago, early North American people began to hunt and fish in the lakes that the moving masses of ice had dug into the earth.

The Dakota are the earliest known Native American tribe in Minnesota. They lived in central and southern Minnesota. The Dakota people separated into small groups throughout the seasons to hunt bison and gather fruits and vegetables. They also tapped trees for maple syrup. They came together in the summer for joyful **rituals** or for gatherings, where they would celebrate and play games. The word "Dakota" means "friend." It refers to the seven different tribal groups that make up the Dakota.

The Dakota depended on the buffalo for food, shelter, and clothing. They moved with the buffalo according to the seasons.

Minnesota's Native Americans Today

Today, more than 60,000 Minnesota Native Americans live in the state's cities and towns and on eleven reservations. In 1968 Native Americans in Minneapolis who were upset about the government's broken promises to Native Americans started the American Indian Movement, or AIM. Today, AIM protects the rights of Native Americans in North America.

The Ojibwe, or Anishinabe, people came to Minnesota from the east thousands of years ago. They lived primarily near Lake Superior and in northeast Minnesota. Anishinabe means "first men." The Ojibwe are known for harvesting wild rice and fishing. But they also hunted deer for their meat and skin, as well as other animals. Today, the Ojibwe are the third-largest Native American tribe in the United States, behind the Cherokee and the Navajo, respectively.

Both the Dakota and Ojibwe lived off what the land gave them. They fought many battles with each other during the 1600s, and the Ojibwe eventually pushed the Dakota south from Lake Mille Lacs to the place now known as Mendota. The Dakota and Ojibwe also fought and traded with the Europeans who were beginning to explore the land in the 1700s.

THE FIRST EUROPEANS

French traders and **voyageurs** were the first Europeans to explore the area that would become Minnesota. In the early 1600s voyageurs traveled from Hudson Bay, through the St. Lawrence River, and to the Great Lakes. The voyageurs were trapping animals for fur and looking for a waterway that went all the way west to China so they could claim it for France.

In 1659 two French traders, Pierre Esprit Radisson and Médart Chouart de Groseilliers, were the first Europeans to travel beyond Lake Superior and meet the Dakota. Radisson and Groseilliers left present-day Montreal, Canada, secretly so they could trade with the Dutch and English instead of the French company that hired them. They thought they would make more money that way. When they returned to Montreal, they hoped to be heroes for finding a new land. Instead, they were fired from their jobs for not buying a license from the French.

Father Louis Hennepin became the first European to see St. Anthony Falls and the area that would later be the Twin Cities. Hennepin wrote best-selling books about North America in 1683 and 1697. They were the first books to describe the land of the Upper Mississippi River.

Then, in 1679, Daniel Duluth journeyed west. Duluth was a French trader, too, but he was on an approved voyage. He met the Dakota, and they took him as far south as Lake Mille Lacs, in what is now central Minnesota. Duluth claimed the land for France and began trading with the Dakota and Ojibwe.

Another explorer who met the Dakota was a Belgian named Father Luis Hennepin. He traveled up the Mississippi River to explore the area in 1679. He was captured by the Dakota and taken to Lake Mille Lacs. Duluth heard about Hennepin and asked the Dakota to let him go. They agreed.

In the early 1700s other French, English, and Spanish explorers came to the area that is now Minnesota. They saw the 100-foot pine trees they could use to build homes, to make furniture, and to make paper. They saw different animals with fur that was valuable all over the world. They saw that Lake Superior and the many large rivers could carry lumber, furs, and other goods to and from the area. They saw there was money to be made in Minnesota.

SETTLING MINNESOTA

The United States became a country in 1776. President Thomas Jefferson, who became president in 1801, saw that the land west of the Mississippi was valuable. In 1803 he bought a large part of it from France. The deal was called the Louisiana Purchase. The United States paid only four cents an acre for an area that would later become thirteen states, including Minnesota.

Pioneers came to settle the land after the Louisiana Purchase. At first they shared the land peacefully with the Dakota and Ojibwe. In the mid-1800s more Americans wanted to come to the area. The U.S. government wanted to sign a **treaty** with the Dakota that gave the United States the land west of the Mississippi. The Dakota were starving because the animals they lived off had become scarce as more people moved into the area and hunted and trapped furs. Though they did not believe land could be bought and sold, the Dakota felt it was only a matter of time before they would be forced off the land. In 1837 the Dakota signed a treaty that gave the United States the land. Less than twenty years later, other treaties with the Dakota and Ojibwe gave almost all of the land the Native Americans lived on to the United States. Thousands of Native Americans were forced to leave the land they thought belonged to everyone.

After treaties were signed in the 1800s, thousands of pioneer farmers came west from the eastern states. **Immigrants** came from Norway, Sweden, Denmark, Germany, and Ireland. Minnesota became a U.S. **territory** in 1849, and shortly afterward, in 1854, a railroad reached the Mississippi River from Chicago. The next year large steam-

Laura Ingalls Wilder

Laura Ingalls Wilder came west with her family in the late 1800s, just like other **settlers.** She traveled from her birthplace in Wisconsin to Kansas and then to Minnesota. In the book *On the Banks of Plum Creek,* she wrote about her life in a sod house on the southern Minnesota prairie. Not much remains of the sod house Wilder grew up in, but people still go to visit the site where it once stood. In fact, there are sod houses built to look exactly like Wilder's all over Minnesota.

boats went through the Soo Canal between Canada and Michigan and made it all the way through Lake Superior to the port of Duluth. That same year the first bridge to span the Mississippi River opened in Minneapolis.

Minnesota had plentiful natural resources to buy and sell. Improvements in transportation made it easier to move lumber, furs, and food from farms in the Minnesota Territory to different parts of the United States and the world. They also made it easier for people to get to Minnesota. Settlers came by train, boat, sled, or wagon. From 1860 to 1900 the population of Minnesota grew more than ten times larger. In 1860 it was 172,023. In 1900 it was 1,751,394.

MINNESOTA BECOMES A STATE

On May 11, 1858, Minnesota became the 32nd state in the **Union.** At that time it was the third-largest state after Texas and California, respectively. Only about 150,000 people lived in Minnesota when it became a state. Today, more than 4.7 million people live in Minnesota.

Charles Lindbergh wrote a book about his famous flight, The Spirit of St. Louis.

FAMOUS PEOPLE

Sinclair Lewis (1885–1951), writer. Sinclair Lewis was born in the small town of Sauk Centre. He was a newspaper writer before he wrote books. He wrote *Main Street,* which is about a small town like Sauk Centre. He was the first American to win the **Nobel Prize for Literature.**

F. Scott Fitzgerald (1896–1940), writer. F. Scott Fitzgerald was born in St. Paul. He wrote novels and short stories. One of his books, *The Great Gatsby,* is considered one of the greatest American books of all time.

Charles Lindbergh (1902–1974), pilot. Charles Lindbergh spent his childhood in Little Falls. He was the first person to fly an airplane solo across the Atlantic Ocean. He did it in a plane called *The Spirit of St. Louis.* He left from New York City and landed in Paris. The flight took 33 hours and 32 minutes.

Statues of Peanuts characters can be found all over the city of St. Paul until they are sold to the highest bidder and become lawn or room ornaments.

Hubert H. Humphrey (1911–1978), vice president. Hubert Humphrey was the vice president of the United States from 1964 to 1968. He served with President Lyndon Johnson. He was also the mayor of Minneapolis twice. Humphrey is known for his support of **civil rights** in the United States and equal opportunity for all people. The Hubert H. Humphrey Metrodome is named in his honor.

Charles Schulz (1922–2000), artist. Charles Schulz created Snoopy and Charlie Brown and the "Peanuts" comic strip. "Peanuts" is one of the most popular comic strips in history and has appeared in more than 2,000 newspapers for more than 50 years.

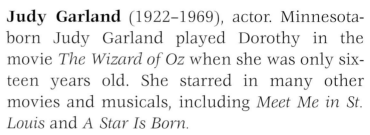

In The Wizard of Oz, *the character Dorothy was from Kansas, but Judy Garland was from Grand Rapids, Minnesota.*

Judy Garland (1922–1969), actor. Minnesota-born Judy Garland played Dorothy in the movie *The Wizard of Oz* when she was only sixteen years old. She starred in many other movies and musicals, including *Meet Me in St. Louis* and *A Star Is Born.*

Bob Dylan (1941–   ), musician. Bob Dylan is considered one of the most important American figures in folk and rock music. His **protest** songs from the 1960s, such as "Blowin' in the Wind" and "The Times They Are A-Changin'" helped rally people against the **Vietnam War** and for **civil rights.** Some of Dylan's songs, such as "Girl from the North Country" and "Highway 61," talk about life in northeast Minnesota, where he is from.

Prince (1958–   ), musician. Prince is a popular rock musician who taught himself guitar, drums, and piano. His movie, *Purple Rain,* was made in his hometown of Minneapolis. He started his own recording studio in Minnesota called Paisley Park.

Briana Scurry (1971–   ), soccer player. Having grown up in Dayton, goalkeeper Briana Scurry is the only women's national team member to play 100 soccer matches for the United States. During the matches of the 1999 World Cup, she played every minute of every game.

In the final 1999 World Cup match against China, goalkeeper Briana Scurry saved a penalty kick during a shootout and helped the United States win the World Cup.

Land of 10,000 Lakes

One of Minnesota's many nicknames is Land of 10,000 Lakes. This nickname is even on many of the state's license plates. Actually, there are about 12,000 lakes in Minnesota larger than ten **acres**.

Because of its lakes, Minnesota has about 90,000 miles of shoreline—more than the ocean states of California, Florida, and Hawaii combined. At least one in six Minnesotans own a boat. More people in Minnesota own boats than in any other state.

LAKE COUNTRY

Two areas in Minnesota are so covered with lakes that Minnesotans call them Lake Country. One is the Boundary Waters Canoe Area Wilderness, which covers more than 1 million acres in northern Minnesota and contains more than 2,000 lakes and streams. Motorboats are not allowed in the Boundary Waters. Instead, visitors paddle canoes from lake to lake through connecting streams or carry canoes between lakes on land trails called portages.

The other lake-filled area is Voyageurs National Park, northwest of the Boundary Waters. The park includes 29

Minnesota's lakes cover nearly 5,000 square miles—about the size of Connecticut.

lakes and more than 500 **beaver ponds,** most connected by streams. The Ojibwe traveled these lakes in birch bark canoes. During the 1700s French-Canadian voyageurs explored these lakes, trapping beavers, foxes, bears, wolves, and other animals for their fur. The voyageurs used the chain of lakes to get the furs to the Great Lakes and then on to Europe and Asia. Today Voyageurs National Park, at 218,200 **acres,** is the largest water-based park in the United States. It is also the oldest water-based national park, established in 1975.

How the Water Flows

Minnesota is unique in that the waters of its rivers and streams flow in three different directions. The way the land lies determines the direction of the water flow. Water drains north from the central part of the state into the Rainy River and Lake of the Woods, and eventually to Hudson Bay in Canada. Water drains east from the central part of the state to the St. Louis River and Lake Superior, and eventually to the Atlantic Ocean. Most of Minnesota's waters drain south from the central part of the state into the Mississippi River, the longest river in North America. In fact, the source, or beginning, of the Mississippi is in Minnesota at Lake Itasca. The river begins as a trickle you can walk across. By the time the river spills into the Gulf of Mexico, the Mississippi River is between 3,000 and 5,000 feet wide and 12 feet deep.

Minnesota's State Government

Like the U.S. government, Minnesota has three branches of government: the legislative branch, the executive branch, and the judicial branch.

Minnesota has a constitution, or plan of government, that states the laws and freedoms in the state, such as freedom of the press and freedom of religion. The constitution was **adopted** when Minnesota became a state in 1858. It is based on the Constitution of the United States.

LEGISLATIVE BRANCH

Minnesota's legislative branch makes the state's laws. This branch consists of two parts: the senate and the house of representatives. There are 67 senators in the senate and 134 representatives in the house of representatives. The voters of Minnesota elect the members of the legislature. Senators serve for four years. Representatives serve for two years. There are no limits to how many terms a Minnesota state senator or representative can serve.

The house of representatives and the senate work together at the state capitol in St. Paul and are called the General Assembly. They both make

Minnesota legislators serve in this chamber in the state capitol, which opened in 1905.

25

Political Parties

A political party is a group of people who have the same ideas about government. The two biggest political parties in the United States are the Republican Party and the Democratic Party. Minnesota is unique in that its Democratic Party is called the Democratic Farm Labor (DFL) Party. The DFL is a combination of the Democratic Party and another party—the Farm-Labor Party. The Farm-Labor Party formed in the late 1800s to help farmers and workers get their needs heard by the legislature. The Farm-Labor Party combined with the Democratic Party in 1944.

Minnesota's laws, and they come up with ideas for new laws called bills. Bills are discussed in public meetings that all Minnesotans can attend. For a bill to become law, a majority, or just over half, of the people in the senate and the house have to agree on it. Then the bill goes to the executive branch.

EXECUTIVE BRANCH

The executive branch carries out the laws and runs the state from day to day. The governor is the head of this branch. One of the main jobs of the governor is to make bills from the legislature into laws. He or she can sign a bill and make it a law, or **veto** the bill and send it back to the legislative branch.

Minnesota's Wrestler Governor

One of Minnesota's most famous governors is Jesse Ventura. Before he was governor from 1998 to 2002, he was a professional wrestler who wore sparkly outfits and had long blond hair. Minnesotans elected Ventura because they wanted a big change. Most people believe his biggest accomplishment was showing that the government is open to everyone.

Executive Branch

Governor and Lt. Governor
(four-year term)

Carries out the laws of the state

Legislative Branch

General Assembly

House of Representatives	Senate
134 Representatives (two-year term)	67 Senators (four-year term)

Makes laws for the state

Judicial Branch

Supreme Court
7 Justices (six-year term)

Court of Appeals
Judges (eight-year term)

District Courts
Judges (six-year term)

Conciliation Courts
Judges (four-year term)

Explains laws of the state

The governor gets help from the lieutenant governor, the second-highest state official, and from members of the **cabinet.** The voters of Minnesota elect the governor and lieutenant governor to a term of four years. The governor chooses the rest of the people in the cabinet, including the leaders of government departments that handle money, health, and the environment.

JUDICIAL BRANCH

Minnesota's judicial branch includes its court system. The courts interpret the state's laws. There are four courts. **Conciliation** courts are the lowest courts. Conciliation courts make decisions on disagreements between people in which less than $7,500 is involved. District courts make decisions on larger disagreements and on criminal cases. District courts also hear cases from conciliation courts on **appeal.** The court of appeals hears all cases that are not solved from conciliation court. The Minnesota Supreme Court is the highest court in the state. The people of the state elect Supreme Court justices for six-year terms.

Minnesota's Culture

Minnesota's **culture** comes from the seasons and weather, the features of Minnesota's geography, and the traditions of the various people who live in the state.

CELEBRATING THE SEASONS

Minnesotans celebrate winter. They snowshoe and snowmobile, ice skate and ice fish, ski, and even sleep in tents in the winter. In St. Paul and Minneapolis, people hold giant winter festivals. From Thanksgiving to Christmas, the streets of Minneapolis come alive with the Holidazzle Parade. Spectators gather every evening during this time to watch dancers, bands, and lighted floats from all over Minnesota wind their way through the downtown area. In St. Paul the Winter Carnival has been celebrated since 1886, when an out-of-town newspaper writer said the city was too cold for human beings. Now, for a few weeks every January, thousands march in parades, ride in dogsleds, slide down a snow slide, compete in winter sports such as speed skating and curling, and sometimes build giant ice castles.

The Minnesota State Fair gets about 1.8 million visitors during the ten days it is open—as many people as the populations of Maine and Alaska put together.

Castles of Ice

Building an ice castle for the Winter Carnival has been a St. Paul tradition since the first one was built in 1886. The castles are not built every year but are saved for special occasions, such as when Minnesota hosted the Super Bowl in 1992. Some of the ice castles are built with elevators and stereos!

Summer also is filled with outdoor celebrations. In the 1800s on the Minnesota prairie, farms and people were miles apart. Fairs helped bring people together. At today's fairs people sample different foods and inspect flowers harvested from gardens. Farm children show animals they have groomed, cleaned, and fed in the hope that they will win a blue ribbon. The largest celebration of all is the Minnesota State Fair, which is held in St. Paul. It is the second-largest state fair in the United States.

CELEBRATING THE LAKES

Minnesotans like to cool off by visiting some of Minnesota's lakes during the hot and sticky days of summer. Going to the lake means swimming, boating, relaxing with a book or two, and fishing. Minnesotans enjoy fishing for walleye, pike, trout, muskie, sunfish, and other types of fish. Fishing is done in all seasons. In winter holes are drilled in the lake for ice fishing.

Minneapolis is known as the "City of Lakes." Since 1940 it has held a festival called Aquatennial every July to celebrate Minnesota's fun with water. People build sandcastles, race boats made from milk cartons, and, of course, fish. More than 800,000 people celebrate Aquatennial each year.

Pow Wows celebrate the history, customs, and contributions of Native American tribes.

CELEBRATING HERITAGE

Immigrants have brought a rich heritage to Minnesota. In 1900 most Minnesotans were German or **Scandinavian** immigrants. Germans brought their religious heritage as **Lutherans.** Scandinavians brought **Nordic skiing** to Minnesota.

After the **Vietnam War** in the 1970s, more than 20,000 **Hmong** refugees from Laos and Cambodia settled in St. Paul. During the 1990s more than 40,000 **Hispanics** came to live in towns and cities in Minnesota. Recently, thousands of Eastern Europeans have moved to the state, as have thousands of immigrants from African nations.

The foods, traditions, and ways of life of these immigrant groups are celebrated with a variety of festivals. For example, the Hmong people celebrate the Hmong New Year in St. Paul in late November or early December. More than 150,000 Hmong people live in the United States, with the largest U.S. urban Hmong population living in St. Paul.

Minnesota's Native Americans celebrate their culture with Pow Wows throughout the state. Pow Wows are a tradition started thousands of years ago, where a tribe would gather to celebrate, make decisions, and trade goods. At today's Pow Wows, Native American performers dance, sing, drum, and tell stories in the traditions of their tribes. Artists sell native art and jewelry. Traditional clothes are worn by dancers, such as the jingle dress, which has up to 700 triangle-shaped jingle bells sewn onto it.

Minnesota's Food

From hot dish to wild rice, Minnesota's food is dictated by the climate and the variety of ethnic groups in the state.

HOT DISH

One of Minnesota's most famous food traditions is hot dish. Hot dish is a warm hearty meal usually made with meat, potatoes, and vegetables. There are hundreds of different kinds of hot dish, such as Tater Tot Hot Dish and Tuna Noodle Hot Dish. However, all share one important fact: hot dish is cooked in one dish.

WILD RICE AND LUTEFISK

Some food traditions in Minnesota are connected to the people who cook and eat them. Minnesota wild rice looks different than white rice—it has a black husk on the outside. For thousands of years Native Americans in Minnesota have harvested this wild rice from **rice paddies** along Minnesota's lakes using canoes made of birch

Hot dish is so popular in Minnesota that entire cookbooks are devoted to hot dish recipes.

Wild Rice Salad

This is one of Minnesota's most popular wild rice dishes. **Be sure to have an adult work the stovetop for you.**

Ingredients

1 cup	wild rice
2 cups	diced and cooked chicken
1½ cups	green grapes, sliced in half
1 cup	sliced water chestnuts
¾ cup	mayonnaise
1 cup	cashews

Cook rice according to package directions. Drain well. Cool to room temperature. Add chicken, grapes, water chestnuts, and mayonnaise. Toss with a fork. Cover and chill. Just before eating, add cashews. Makes six servings.

bark. **Norwegians** and others in Minnesota eat lutefisk, a dish made of any boiled white fish and served with butter.

Today, Minnesotans' food choices are growing as people from different cultures move to the state. Asians, Hispanics, Russians, and Africans are adding different spices, pastas, and vegetables to the meat and potatoes Minnesotans have traditionally eaten.

Minnesota's Folklore and Legends

Legends and folklore are stories that are not totally true but are often based on bits of truth. These stories helped people understand things that could not be easily explained. They also taught lessons to younger generations. All peoples have passed down stories as part of their culture. Minnesota is home to unique stories about the land and people who may have lived there.

KENSINGTON RUNE STONE

Were French fur traders really the first Europeans to see Minnesota? Many people believe the **Vikings** were the Europeans who first set foot in Minnesota. Some Minnesotans believe that a message carved on a 200-pound stone in the central Minnesota town of Kensington proves the Vikings set foot in Minnesota 400 years before the French.

The words carved on the Kensington Runestone tell how Vikings came to

A Swedish farmer named Olaf Ohman discovered the runestone on his property in 1898. It is 31 inches long, 16 inches wide, and 6 inches thick.

Minnesota through Canada and the Red River. Most people believe the stone is a hoax, or practical joke, but no one knows for sure.

PAUL BUNYAN

He was so big, he wore wagon wheels for buttons. When he walked around Minnesota, his footprints left giant holes that filled with water and became Minnesota's lakes. His name was Paul Bunyan, and he was the biggest, strongest lumberjack who ever lived. Or so the story goes. Real lumberjacks cutting trees in the long Minnesota winters told "tall tales;" they would exaggerate the hardships of their work and turn them into funny stories.

One tale told of the year when winter was so cold and long it was called the Year of Two Winters. The snow was so deep that Paul had to dig down to get to the trees he needed to cut. It was so cold the coffee froze while it was still hot, and when the men spoke, their words froze in midair. When winter finally thawed, so did the words, and there was a terrible chatter for weeks.

Where Is Paul?

If you drive around northern Minnesota, you will probably see Paul Bunyan. Minnesota is home to 26 Paul Bunyan statues—one of the largest is in Bemidji. There are also statues of his blue ox, Babe, and his belongings, including his shovel, mailbox, and harmonica. Stories about Paul Bunyan were printed in advertisements for the Red River Lumber Company in Akeley, Minnesota, and that helped spread the word about the world's largest lumberjack.

Minnesota's Sports Teams

Sports are popular in Minnesota. All different kinds of sports are played in all different kinds of weather.

PROFESSIONAL SPORTS

The Minnesota **Vikings** are Minnesota's National Football League team. Vikings football games are played in the Metrodome, an indoor sports stadium in Minneapolis.

The Minnesota Twins play baseball in the Metrodome, too. The team is named after the Twin Cities of Minneapolis and St. Paul. The Twins won the World Series in 1987 and 1991 with baseball hall-of-famer Kirby Puckett. The 1991 World Series, in which the Twins beat the Atlanta Braves four games to three, was one of the most closely contested in baseball history. Five games were decided by one run, and all five were decided in the last at-bat.

The Minnesota Timberwolves play in the National Basketball Association (NBA) at the Target Center in Minneapolis. Led by forward Kevin Garnett, the Timberwolves have made the NBA playoffs from 1999 to 2003.

The Vikings have been to the Super Bowl four times and tied a record for regular season wins with fifteen in 1998.

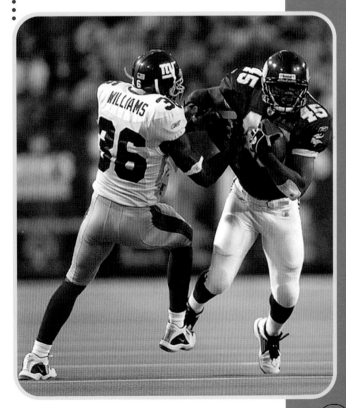

The Minnesota Wild play hockey in the Xcel Energy Center in downtown St. Paul. The Wild are Minnesota's newest professional sports team. The Wild joined the National Hockey League (NHL) in 2000 and made the conference finals in 2003.

COLLEGE SPORTS

The University of Minnesota at the Twin Cities is the state's largest college and is in the Big Ten Conference. The college has won five men's ice hockey national championships, including back-to-back titles in 2002 and 2003. The University of Minnesota at Duluth has won three women's ice hockey championships. More than 150 Minnesotans have played in the NHL or on men's or women's Olympic hockey teams.

In 2001 more than 110,000 people watched the boys high school ice hockey championship games in the Xcel Energy Center.

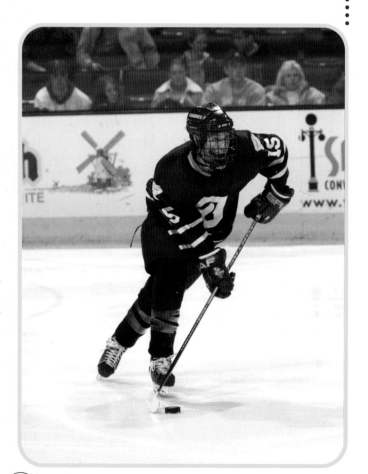

HIGH SCHOOL ICE HOCKEY

Minnesota is known for ice hockey, and the boys high school state championship tournament is a unique sporting event. It began in 1945 and since then more than four million people have attended the games. Minnesota has produced such players as Neal Broten, who won a gold medal for the United States in the 1980 Winter Olympics.

Minnesota's Businesses and Products

In the 1600s there was fur trading. Then, in the 1800s, there was logging. Today, many different industries, including farming and health care industries, do business in Minnesota.

Some farms are family owned. There are about 80,000 farms in Minnesota, averaging 364 acres each.

FARM PRODUCTS

Before 1950 most Minnesotans lived on farms or in small towns. Today, more than 50 percent of the people live in the Twin Cities. Now, there are 30,000 fewer farms in the state, and the farms still operating are, on average, 20 percent bigger and owned by corporations instead of families. But farming is still an important business in the state.

Minnesota is one of the top five producers in the nation of more than ten different crops. Minnesota is first in growing sweet corn, green peas, and sugar beets, and second in growing wild rice. Minnesota is first in the nation in making American cheese and second in raising turkeys.

MINING

Northern Minnesota has been the top U.S. producer of **iron ore** since it was found in the state in the 1880s. Today, 75 percent of U.S. ore comes from Minnesota. Iron ore is a rock that contains iron and other minerals and is used to make iron and steel. So much iron ore is found in an area of northern Minnesota that it is known as the "Iron Range." The iron there is close to the surface of the earth, not deep down, so miners do not need to dig tunnels to get it. Instead, they dig gigantic holes right out of the top of the earth, creating small canyons in the landscape. This kind of mining is called open-pit mining. The town of Hibbing is home to the largest open-pit iron mine in the world.

Today, much of the iron ore has been mined. Now taconite is mined in Minnesota instead. Taconite is a rock similar to iron ore but with less iron in it. Scientists in Minnesota helped invent a way to get the iron ore out of taconite. Large chunks of taconite rock are ground down to a powder. Then, giant magnets pull the iron out of the powder. The iron is then pressed and baked into taconite pellets. Lake Superior cargo ships take the taconite pellets to steel mills in the eastern United States. About 24 million tons of taconite come from Minnesota's mines every year.

The Iron Man Statue in Chisholm was built as a tribute to the iron ore miners of northeastern Minnesota. It stands 81 feet high and is the third largest free-standing statue in the nation.

The Mayo Clinic

In 1883 a tornado ripped through Rochester, Minnesota. Many people were hurt, and there was no hospital to treat them. Dr. William Mayo and Dr. Charles Mayo, with the help of local nuns, treated the injured in hotels instead. A few years later the brothers and the nuns built the first hospital in southeastern Minnesota,

Saint Mary's hospital, and the brothers started the world-famous Mayo Clinic. The clinic is known for its research on cancer, diabetes, and weight loss, and for the teamwork doctors use to help patients.

FAMOUS MINNESOTA COMPANIES

Minnesota Mining and Manufacturing, more commonly known as 3M, invented Post-it notes, Scotch tape, and masking tape. Five businessmen from northern Minnesota started 3M nearly 100 years ago. Today, 3M has more than $16 billion in sales worldwide.

Minnesotan John Pillsbury helped turn a flour mill in Minneapolis into a large food company by inventing refrigerated cookie dough, the Bundt cake, and the Pillsbury Doughboy. Minnesotan and railroad ticket agent Richard Sears founded Sears, Roebuck, and Company when, in 1886, he bought a shipment of unwanted watches and sold them up and down the railroad line.

Attractions and Landmarks

From the serene lake chains of the north to the high **bluffs** and scenic rivers of the southeast to the vast prairies of the west to the vibrant Twin Cities, there are many things to see and do in Minnesota.

FUN AT THE MALL

The Mall of America in Bloomington is the biggest mall in the United States. Each year, more people visit it than Disney World, the Grand Canyon, and Elvis Presley's home put together. In fact, more than 250 million people have visited the mall since it opened in 1992—that is about the population of the entire United States! Minnesotans like to call it the Mega Mall.

The mall is 4.2 million square feet—about the size of 78 football fields—and contains more than 520 stores. There are 50 restaurants, 8 nightclubs, and 14 movie screens. The world's largest indoor amusement park, Camp Snoopy, is in the middle of the mall.

The Mall of America is not just for shopping. Inside you will find a giant tunnel-like aquarium, a college, a high school, a wedding chapel, a post office, and a police station.

FUN IN THE TWIN CITIES

Minneapolis and St. Paul are home to hundreds of parks. One of the most visited is the Minneapolis **Sculpture** Garden. Built in 1988, the eleven-acre park is the largest sculpture garden in the United States. There, people can find a famous Twin Cities **landmark:** the giant Spoonbridge and Cherry sculpture.

The husband-and-wife artist team of Claes Oldenburg and Coosje Van Bruggen made the Spoonbridge and Cherry sculpture between 1985 and 1988.

At the Science Museum of Minnesota, visitors can watch a movie from the world's largest movie projector—a 7,000-watt projector. That is more than 115 times stronger than the light bulb in most lamps found in homes.

FUN IN THE OUTDOORS

Minnesota is home to 66 state parks, 57 state forests, and 2 national forests—the Superior National Forest in the northeast part of the state and the Chippewa National Forest in the north central part of the state. The Boundary Waters Canoe Area Wilderness and Voyageurs National Park has more than 1,000 lakes and 1,500 miles of canoe routes. It can be found in

At the Science Museum of Minnesota, the exhibits include such things as an Egyptian mummy, a real Mississippi River tugboat, and the largest complete triceratops on display in the world.

Minnesota has more than 21,000 miles of trails for hiking, biking, skiing, snowmobiling, and horseback riding.

the northern part of the state. *National Geographic* magazine named it one of 50 destinations of a lifetime. In Minnesota, you can also find sections of a national hiking trail called the North Country Trail. When the trail is finished, hikers will be able to walk on one trail across the northern states from coast to coast.

There are two National Monuments in Minnesota. At the Pipestone National Monument in southwestern Minnesota, people can visit the place where Native Americans mined pink and red stone for carving pipes. Grand Portage National Monument near the Canadian border in the northeast marks the historical center of the fur trade, Minnesota's first industry. Tourists can find Ojibwe and

The Root Beer Lady

Dorothy Molter was a nurse who lived in the Boundary Waters Canoe Area Wilderness from the 1950s until she died in 1986. She was known for her homemade root beer. People on canoe trips loved to stop by for a bottle or two. When the U.S. government passed a bill that said the Boundary Waters was protected wilderness, they asked all the people who lived there to move. But Dorothy Molter's friends signed petitions to keep her there, so the government let her stay. Even though she saw about 6,000 visitors a year, she was the only person who lived in the Boundary Waters' 1 million acres of forest.

Places to See in Minnesota

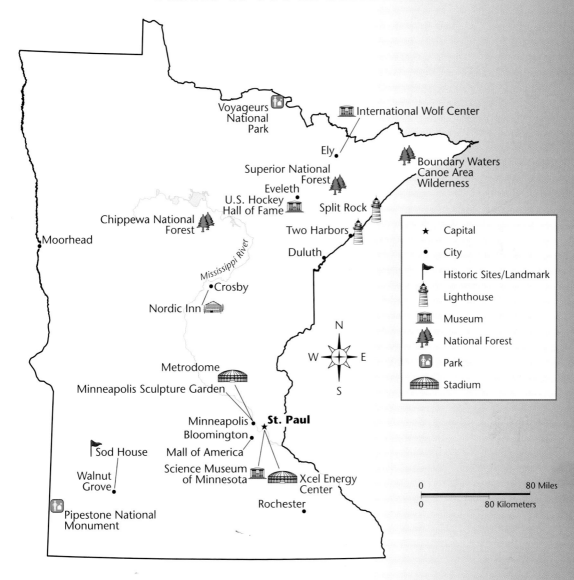

voyageur **artifacts,** as well as replicas of birch bark canoes that the Ojibwe and voyageurs used.

FUN IN SMALL TOWNS

At the Nordic Inn in Crosby in central Minnesota, visitors can eat with their hands, cut soap from a big soap block with an ax, and sleep in a boat, just like the **Vikings** did. At Moorhead in western Minnesota, people

Lake Wobegon

Lake Wobegon is probably Minnesota's most famous small town. But it is not a real town. Garrison Keillor, who grew up in Anoka, invented Lake Wobegon. He has been writing about this made-up town for 30 years, and he reads his stories on a radio show called *A Prairie Home Companion.*

can see a replica of a Viking ship that some Minnesotans built. These same people sailed it from Lake Superior to Norway in the summer of 1980.

In the city of Eveleth in northern Minnesota, people can visit the U.S. Hockey Hall of Fame. It has the world's longest hockey stick, which measures 107 feet long. Tourists can also visit the International Wolf Center in Ely. The largest wolf population in the lower 48 states lives near Ely, and the center studies the wolves and educates people about them. Along Lake Superior, people can visit lighthouses at Two Harbors and Split Rock. These lighthouses saved ships from running aground on the lake's rocky shore.

Map of Minnesota

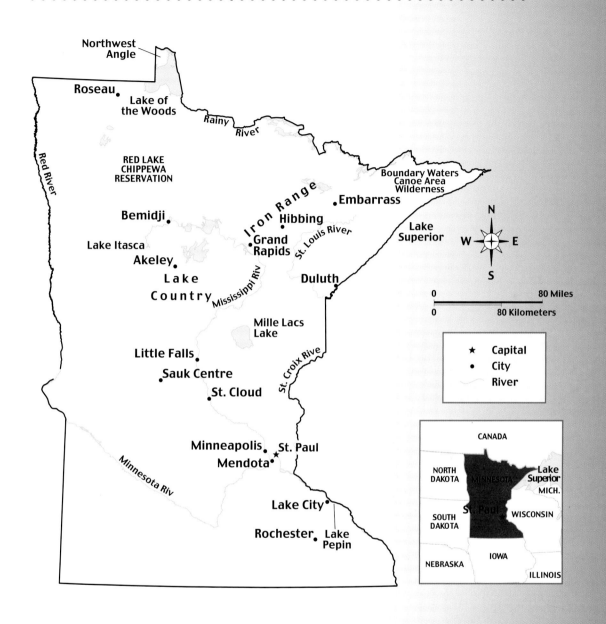

Northwest Angle

Roseau

Lake of the Woods

Rainy River

Red River

RED LAKE CHIPPEWA RESERVATION

Bemidji

Lake Itasca

Akeley

Lake Country

Iron Range

Grand Rapids

Hibbing

Embarrass

Boundary Waters Canoe Area Wilderness

St. Louis River

Lake Superior

Mississippi Riv

Duluth

Mille Lacs Lake

St. Croix Rive

Little Falls

Sauk Centre

St. Cloud

Minneapolis

St. Paul

Mendota

Minnesota Riv

Lake City

Rochester

Lake Pepin

N
W E
S

| 0 | 80 Miles |
| 0 | 80 Kilometers |

★	Capital
•	City
～	River

CANADA

NORTH DAKOTA

MINNESOTA

Lake Superior

MICH.

SOUTH DAKOTA

St. Paul

WISCONSIN

NEBRASKA

IOWA

ILLINOIS

Glossary

acres a unit of area used to measure land. 1 acre = 43,560 square feet

adopted voted to accept

affirmative action actively trying to improve life for minorities and women

agate a kind of crystal with colored stripes or bands

appeal to take a case to a higher court

artifacts the remains of buildings, pottery, bones, and other items left behind by ancient people

basilica a Catholic church that has been given special privileges by the pope

beaver ponds a small, still body of water where beavers live

bluffs steep cliffs

cabinet a group of people chosen by a leader to help him or her run a government

civil rights the rights of U.S. citizens given by the Constitution

conciliation agreeing on something

continental one of the 48 lower states; the part of the United States on the North American continent

culture the behaviors, art, foods, and beliefs of a community

extreme when something is the most it can be in two different ways, such as hot and cold

fungus a plant material that reproduces in spores and lives off other plants

glacier a giant sheet of moving ice

heritage the traditions of a community or people

Hispanics a group of people from Spain or Latin America

Hmong a group of people who originally came from Laos and Cambodia

humid lots of moisture in the air

immigrants people who leave one country to settle in another

iron ore a kind of metal from the ground that can be made into iron and steel

landmark a feature important to a place

Lutherans members of the Lutheran church, a Christian religion

musket a large, heavy gun carried by a soldier

Nobel Prize for Literature an international prize that is awarded once a year to honor the lifetime achievement of a writer.

Nordic skiing cross-country skiing where skiers slide with their skis on flat land as if they were running

Norwegians people from Norway

peninsula a piece of land that juts into a body of water

pioneers people who settled in new territories before they became states

port a city built beside a body of water where ships come in and out

protest acting against something

quartz a shiny rock made up of crystals

rice paddies a flooded area where rice is grown

rituals ceremonies

Scandinavians people from the countries of Norway, Sweden, or Denmark

sculpture three-dimensional artwork

settlers people who came to a state first

stoic not easily excited, showing neither pain nor pleasure

symbol something that stands for something else

territory a land that has a governor but is not yet a state

treaty a written agreement

Union the northern states in the Civil War

veto to prevent a bill from being passed

Vietnam War a war the United States helped fight against North Vietnam during the late 1960s and early 1970s

Vikings Scandinavians who traveled to North America in ships more than 1,000 years ago

voyageurs French fur traders who came to Minnesota in the 1600s

More Books to Read

• •

Grabowski, John F. *Minnesota Vikings.* San Diego, Calif.: Lucent, 2002.

Johnston, Patricia Condon. *Minnesota: Portrait of the Land and Its People.* Helena, Mont.: American Geographic Publishing, 1987.

Ringsak, Russ. *Minnesota Curiosities.* Guilford, Conn.: Globe Pequot Press, 2003.

Uschan, Michael V. *Jesse Ventura.* San Diego, Calif.: Lucent, 2001.

Wilder, Laura Ingalls. *On the Banks of Plum Creek.* New York: HarperTrophy, 1973.

Index

About the Author

Stephanie Ash is a writer who lives in Minnesota. She loves to walk over the source of the Mississippi River in Itasca State Park and to camp near the river in southeast Minnesota. Her favorite Minnesotans are her own two boys, Christian and Charlie.